D1444015

Science Concepts SECOND SERIES

Weather and Climate

Alvin Silverstein, Virginia Silverstein, and Laura Silverstein Nunn

Twenty-First Century Books

Minneapolis

Text copyright © 2008 by Alvin Silverstein, Virginia Silverstein, and Laura
Silverstein Nunn

Twenty-First Century Books
A division of Lerner Publishing Group, Inc.
241 First Avenue North
Minneapolis, MN 55401 U.S.A.

Website address: www.lernerbooks.com

Library of Congress Cataloging-in-Publication Data

Silverstein, Alvin.
    Weather and climate / by Alvin Silverstein, Virginia Silverstein, and
Laura Silverstein Nunn. — Rev. ed.
        p.   cm. — (Science Concepts)
    Includes bibliographical references and index.
    ISBN 978-0-8225-6796-7 (lib. bdg. : alk. paper)
    1. Weather—Juvenile literature. 2. Meteorology—Juvenile literature.
3. Climatic changes—Juvenile literature. I. Silverstein, Virginia B. II. Nunn,
Laura Silverstein. III. Title.
QC981.3.S55 2008
551.5—dc22   2007003188

Manufactured in the United States of America
1 2 3 4 5 6 – DP – 13 12 11 10 09 08

Contents

chapter one

How's the Weather?

What's one of the first things you think about when you wake up in the morning? Is it the weather? Do you wonder if it will be cold or warm outside? Sunny or rainy? What about snow? Depending on the weather, you decide what clothes to wear—a heavy coat, a light jacket, or no jacket at all. How about boots and an umbrella?

Every day, you and people all over the world make plans according to the weather. In fact, cable and satellite-TV services dedicate a whole channel to nothing but weather. It's not surprising. Weather affects your life in many ways. Rain can stop a baseball game or cancel your travel plans for a weekend at the beach. Snow may make roads dangerous to drive, but it may be great news for skiers.

Farmers worry about the weather because their crops need a balance of sun and rain. While you might be happy to have sunshine day after day, plants need rain to grow. Without rain, we would have nothing to eat. The grass would be brown all year round, and flowers would shrivel up.

Your house is most likely built according to the

Rain can affect an outdoor sporting event, as it did when storm clouds gathered and rain fell on this tennis tournament in Australia.

type of weather in your area. If your winters are cold and your summers are hot, your house should be well insulated to keep out the heat or cold, depending on the season. In very rainy places, houses are built with steep, pointed roofs so that the rain can run off easily.

Animals are also affected by the weather. Bears, for instance, put on extra pounds during the summer and fall so they can sleep throughout the winter. During this deep sleep, called hibernation, their body feeds off their fat reserves

Black bears like this one hibernate through the cold winter months in North America.

These geese fly in a V formation as they migrate south for the winter.

until springtime. Hibernation is essential to their survival because food becomes scarce during the winter. Other creatures migrate—move to places with more favorable weather conditions—where food is more plentiful. Have you heard geese honking as they fly south for the winter?

Something in the Air

What do people mean when they ask, "How's the weather?" Meteorologists, or scientists who study the weather, explain that it is the condition of the air at a particular time. It may be cold, warm, sunny, foggy, raining, snowing, or sleeting—or usually some combination of these conditions.

All weather occurs in the air, or atmosphere. We cannot see air, but we know it's there. If you wet your finger and hold it out in front of you, it will feel cool. What you feel is the air moving against your finger. Air is a mixture of gases that blankets Earth and makes up the atmosphere.

The atmosphere is never completely dry. It

contains moisture, mostly in the form of an invisible gas called water vapor. The moisture comes from the surface of oceans, lakes, rivers, and other bodies of water where some of the liquid turns into gas. Plants also release water vapor into the air.

The Water Cycle

Water is essential to our weather machine. That's not surprising, since water covers close to three-quarters of our planet. In a process called the water cycle, the sun heats up the oceans—and to a lesser extent, smaller bodies of water—causing large amounts of water to evaporate, or change from a liquid to a vapor. The warm, moist air rises into the atmosphere. As winds carry the moist air away, it begins to cool. Eventually the water is too cool to stay in a vaporous state. It condenses, turning into tiny water droplets and

Weather vs. Climate

Weather is often confused with climate. People may think that when they talk about weather, they are also describing the climate. That's not exactly true. Weather is a condition of the atmosphere from one day to the next. Today is sunny and warm, and tomorrow will be rainy and cool. Climate describes weather conditions in a particular place over a period of years. Phoenix, Arizona, for example, has a warm, dry climate, while Fairbanks, Alaska, has a cold climate much of the year, with plenty of ice and snow.

sometimes freezing as ice crystals. These make up the clouds, mist, and fog that surround Earth. When the drops or crystals become too heavy to stay up in the air, the clouds return water back to Earth as rain, snow, hail, or another form of precipitation to complete the water cycle.

Our Earth has been using the same water for more than three billion years, recycling it from the oceans to the sky and back again.

Nature recycles water between the lands and bodies of water of Earth's surface and the water vapor in the atmosphere. Evaporation and precipitation are important parts of the water cycle.

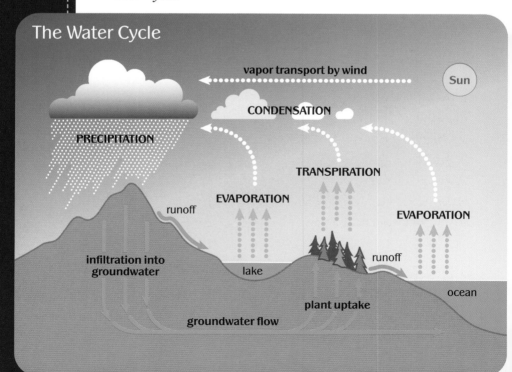

The Water Cycle

vapor transport by wind

Sun

CONDENSATION

PRECIPITATION

TRANSPIRATION

EVAPORATION

runoff

EVAPORATION

infiltration into groundwater

lake

runoff

ocean

plant uptake

groundwater flow

Air in Motion

The air is in constant motion due to energy from the sun. The sun's rays heat the air and Earth's surface beneath it, some places more than others. Oceans hold on to the heat better than land does. Warm air tends to rise, while cool air falls. These air movements cause the atmosphere to swirl and bubble like water heating in a pot on the stove. Cold and warm air masses are constantly moving around the

Moving air masses can sometimes cause stormy weather like this Florida hurricane in 2004.

planet, producing winds. The moving air helps to spread the air heated by sunlight to parts of the world that are not heated as directly. But this is not always a smooth process. Air masses may bump into one another, producing stormy weather—thunderstorms, blizzards, or even violent tornadoes and hurricanes.

Changing Weather, Changing World

Over the ages, weather patterns have changed many times. Imagine a world with winter temperatures all year long and ice

Due to uncommonly warm weather in December 2006, this ski resort in Austria had no snow, therefore no skiers.

and snow always on the ground. Could that really happen? Actually, it has happened several times throughout Earth's history, during ice ages. The lowest temperatures ever reached occurred during the ice ages. Earth has experienced great warmings as well. Places with normally cold winters had a tropical climate. Evidence shows that our planet's climate has cooled and warmed many times—and this fluctuation is still going on.

Today, we seem to be in the midst of a world-wide warming trend—a global warming. Many scientists believe that industrialization is helping to speed up the process. Earth is like a greenhouse.

Certain gases in the atmosphere, such as carbon dioxide, absorb some of the sun's rays, preventing heat from escaping into space. With just the right amount of heat, Earth stays warm and comfortable. But if it gets too hot, the effects could be disastrous. Pollutants produced by homes and industry rise into the atmosphere and add to the greenhouse effect. Many scientists believe that as more "greenhouse gases" in the atmosphere trap heat, Earth will get much warmer. Therefore, reducing and even eliminating pollution has become an important goal in our society.

The better we can predict weather, the better we can prepare ourselves for any changes in the weather. If we could better predict hurricanes and tornadoes, for example, many lives could be saved. Scientists continue to improve devices and techniques for weather forecasting. As the world's population grows and we live in more areas of our planet, predicting the weather may not be a luxury but a necessity.

Earth's Atmosphere

chapter two

On a clear day, the sky seems to go on forever. It's no wonder—the atmosphere stretches more than 600 miles (1,000 kilometers) out into space. The atmosphere's mixture of gases contains about four-fifths nitrogen. The rest is mostly oxygen, along with small amounts of water vapor, carbon dioxide, and several other gases.

Although tiny traces of the atmosphere can be found hundreds of miles above Earth, the pull of gravity has compacted most of the gases into a thin layer only 6 to 10 miles (10 to 16 km) thick. (Gravity is a force that attracts objects to one another. It attracts the atmosphere to Earth and keeps it from drifting off into space.) This relatively thin layer of atmosphere—containing the air that we breathe—is its lowest part, called the troposphere. It makes up about 80 percent of Earth's atmosphere.

Four more layers of atmosphere surround Earth. From the innermost layer outward, they are the stratosphere, the mesosphere, the thermosphere, and the exosphere.

Earth's weather occurs in the troposphere. It has

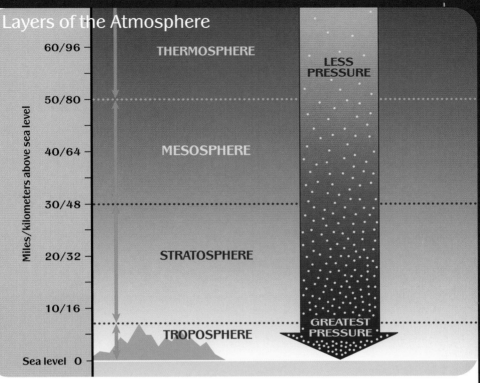

Layers of the Atmosphere

Miles/kilometers above sea level

- 60/96 — THERMOSPHERE
- 50/80
- 40/64 — MESOSPHERE
- 30/48
- 20/32 — STRATOSPHERE
- 10/16
- TROPOSPHERE
- Sea level 0

LESS PRESSURE

GREATEST PRESSURE

Earth's atmosphere is made up of several layers. The lowest layer—the troposphere—is where our weather occurs.

the most water vapor, which is needed to form clouds. Clouds, in turn, produce rain, snow, sleet, and hail. The sun's heat energy sets the air in the troposphere constantly moving and churning, creating a variety of weather conditions. Airline pilots often prefer to fly in the lower stratosphere to avoid bad weather conditions in the underlying troposphere.

The Atmosphere, Our Protector

The atmosphere is essential to all living things. It is a provider and a protector. Life on Earth depends on certain gases in the atmosphere. We take in oxygen when we breathe, and we exhale carbon dioxide. Plants take in oxygen and give off carbon dioxide too. But they also use carbon dioxide to make food for themselves. During food making—a process called photosynthesis—plants produce much more oxygen than they need, and the excess passes out into the atmosphere. Most living things cannot use the nitrogen gas from the atmosphere directly, but they need nitrogen to form important body chemicals. The connecting link is

Earth's atmosphere is just a shallow layer of gas that becomes thinner and fainter the higher you go. This picture, taken by an astronaut, shows the moon peeking over the upper edge of Earth's atmosphere.

provided by bacteria in the soil that can turn nitrogen from the atmosphere into chemicals that plants can use.

The atmosphere protects our planet from the full force of the sun's energy. Most of the sun's rays that reach our planet are absorbed by ozone, a form of oxygen that is present in the upper atmosphere (mostly in the stratosphere). Without this protective shield, Earth's surface would reach boiling temperatures. The atmosphere helps to distribute the warmth of sunlight around the planet and acts as a blanket at night, keeping the heat from escaping too rapidly.

Did You Know?

Earth's original atmosphere was poisonous, with hardly any oxygen. Oxygen increased as plants began to use sunlight and carbon dioxide in the food-making process called photosynthesis. They released oxygen as a by-product. So we can thank simple plants from millions of years ago for our breathable air.

chapter three

The Weather Machine

Heat energy from the sun is the engine that drives our weather machine. Because Earth is curved, the sun's rays heat its surface unevenly. It is hottest at the equator because the rays strike most directly there. Areas around the equator are called the tropics. The sun's rays spread out as they move toward the North and South Poles. The poles are the coldest places on Earth because they get the least direct sunlight.

Land areas absorb and reflect more of the sunlight energy than water does, so the air above the land is warmer than the air above the ocean. These temperature differences lead to movements in the air.

Air on the Move

The air is made up of gas molecules—particles that contain more than one atom. They are far too small to see, even with a microscope. The molecules in cold air move very slowly and condense—squeeze together in a small space. They become heavy and fall toward the ground. The ground absorbs heat from the sun's rays.

A wind storm howls around a camp in the North Pole (above). *The North Pole and South Pole are the coldest places on Earth because they get the least amount of direct sunlight. This rain forest in Venezuela* (below) *is near the equator. Areas near the equator are some of the hottest on Earth because the sun's rays hit them most directly. These areas are also home to the world's tropical rain forests.*

The cold air above the ground then also warms up. As the gas molecules are heated, they start to move very fast. Their kinetic energy—energy of motion—has increased. The moving molecules bang into one another, forcing them to expand (spread out) and rise into the air. Hot-air balloons work by using warm air to push the balloon higher into the air. As the air in the balloon cools down, the balloon starts to fall.

This weather map shows the weather activity around the United States, as well as a cold front, warm front, and stationary front. It also shows the varying temperatures around the country. Blue is cold in the north. Green and yellow in the midsection show moderate temperatures. Orange is in parts of the south, where temperatures are very warm.

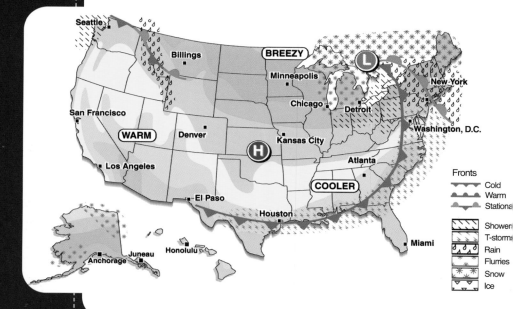

Weather and Climate

As a result of warm air rising and cool air falling, areas of warm and cold air chase one another around. They produce a continuous cycle of movement called convection currents. These patches of cold or warm air constantly moving around the planet create winds. Without winds, temperatures would be constant—hot places would remain hot, and cold places would remain cold. Air that circulates over the entire Earth is called general circulation.

When only one air mass moves over an area, the weather is fair and stable. If two air masses crash into each other, they produce a front, causing disturbances in the atmosphere. When warm air moves into an area of cold air, it is called a warm front. Conversely, cold air that moves into an area of warm air is called a cold front.

Water on the Move

Just as winds are an effective air-circulating system, Earth also has an amazing water-circulating system. The sun's energy heats not only the air and the ground but also the oceans, setting them constantly on the move. Ocean currents move cold and warm water to different parts of Earth. Warm currents move away from the equator, and cool water comes in to replace them. Near the poles, cool currents are replaced by the warm currents. These currents in the oceans also influence the weather on the nearby lands, because winds above the water carry warm or cool air ashore.

Water takes a long time both to absorb heat and to cool down. Therefore, areas near large bodies of water have cooler summers and warmer winters than inland areas.

Two currents that have a strong influence on the weather are the Gulf Stream and the Humboldt Current. The Gulf Stream is a warm-water current that starts in the western Caribbean Sea, passes through the Gulf of Mexico and the Straits of Florida, then flows northeast along the North American coast. The Gulf Stream warms the air above it. When the wind blows, it moves the warm ocean air to other parts of the world including the British Isles and Scandinavia. The Humboldt Current is a cold-water current that flows northward along the west coast of South America, bringing cold-air winds along the way.

Under Pressure

You probably don't feel it, but air is constantly pressing down on you with tremendous force. This pushing force is called air pressure, or atmospheric pressure. Air pressure is the result of billions of air molecules banging into one another as they zoom back and forth. The weight of the total atmosphere is 5.8 quadrillion tons (5.2 quadrillion metric tons)! That comes to about 14.7 pounds for every square inch (about 1 kilogram per sq. centimeter), or about 1 ton (1 metric ton) of weight on your entire body. Why don't you feel such a heavy weight? Because the air pressure inside your body balances the outside pressure.

Air pressure is highest at sea level because the air

is densest there—it contains the most air molecules. If you climb a mountain, the air pressure decreases because the air becomes thinner. (Remember: air molecules spread out at higher levels.) Above 16,400 feet (5,000 meters), the air pressure is so low that breathing becomes difficult. That is why mountain climbers need to wear oxygen masks when they climb the highest peaks. Jet planes are pressurized—extra air is pumped into their sealed cabins—so that the passengers and crew have enough oxygen to breathe. Oxygen masks are provided for an emergency drop in air pressure.

Why Do Your Ears Pop?

Have you ever been in an airplane and noticed that your ears start to pop as the plane climbs into the sky? That's because there is a change in air pressure. The same thing may happen when you ride up in an elevator. At sea level, the air pressure is the same outside and inside your body. As altitude increases, with fewer atmospheric gas molecules, the air pressure drops. Your ears may pop because the air trapped inside your ears, at a higher pressure than the air outside your body, makes your eardrums bulge outward. Chewing gum during a takeoff prompts you to swallow saliva, opening the tubes that connect the breathing passages to your ears and equalizing the pressures painlessly. A similar thing happens when the plane comes in for a landing and the pressure inside your ears is lower than the air pressure outside.

Air pressure also varies with the temperature. Near the poles, where it is coldest, the air molecules are close together and the air pressure is high. At the equator, where it is much warmer, the air is less dense and the pressure is lower.

Air pressure is an important factor in weather. You may have heard weather forecasters talk about high-pressure systems and low-pressure systems. In high-pressure systems, or highs, winds blow from high altitudes down toward Earth's surface. Air becomes drier as it falls, so the weather becomes stable and fair. High-pressure systems usually stay in one place. Some, called migratory high-pressure systems, move west to east.

Low-pressure systems, or lows, are more unstable. With a swirling motion, warm-air currents rise into the sky forming clouds along the way. Air pressure tends to push air from high-pressure areas to low-pressure areas. When the two pressure systems collide, they produce a weather front, where thunderstorms or other storm systems may occur.

Air pressure is measured with an instrument called an aneroid barometer. The barometer shows what kind of pressure system is in the air. Barometer

Did You Know?
If you were at the top of Mount Everest, you would not be able to boil an egg because the air pressure is too low. There are not enough molecules at that high elevation, so water would not get hot enough to boil.

readings are measured in millibars (mb). At sea level, normal air pressure is about 1,013 mb. In a high-pressure system, a barometer may read 1,040 mb. The pressure may drop to 950 mb in a low-pressure system. Weather forecasters use barometer readings to predict the weather.

Which Way the Wind Blows

An aneroid barometer measures air pressure with the accuracy needed by meteorologists.

The old saying "Every wind has its weather" is true! Different kinds of winds bring different types of weather. Some winds bring sunny skies. Others bring rain or snow. We can learn a lot about the weather by finding out which way the wind blows. Air masses over land are dry, while those over the oceans are moist. Air masses from the tropics are warm, and air masses from the poles are cold. So in the United States, for example, winds that blow from the north, called north winds, bring cold weather; winds that come from the west, called west winds, bring rain.

Winds generally move from high-pressure areas, such as the polar regions, toward low-pressure areas around the

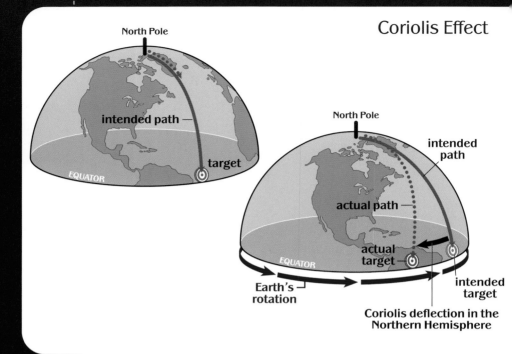

Coriolis Effect

North Pole

intended path —

target

EQUATOR

North Pole

intended path

actual path —

actual target —

EQUATOR

Earth's rotation

intended target

Coriolis deflection in the Northern Hemisphere

When you draw a line from the North Pole to the equator, the line will shift as the globe is turned to simulate Earth's rotation. This shift is called the Coriolis effect.

equator. Because Earth rotates, or spins, the winds cannot move in a direct north-south direction. Winds blowing from the poles toward the equator are shifted westward by Earth's rotation. This is called the Coriolis effect, after a French physics professor, Gaspard-Gustave de Coriolis, who explained in 1835 how it worked.

Some winds, called prevailing winds, tend to blow in the same direction all year round. Others blow only in certain seasons, at certain times of the day, in certain local areas, or during storms.

Prevailing Winds

Long ago, sailors knew that prevailing winds could help them get across the oceans. Prevailing winds make a pattern of six bands around the globe, like stripes on a flag. Within each band, or belt, the prevailing winds all blow in the same general direction. The two belts just north and south of the equator are called trade winds. The next belts both north and south are called prevailing westerlies, and the belts closest to the poles are the polar easterlies. Easterlies and westerlies refer to the direction from which the winds are coming.

Warm air rises from the hot equatorial regions and moves toward the poles. Cooler air sweeps down to replace it, producing the trade winds. Moving toward the equator, these winds are shifted westward over the rotating surface of Earth, so they blow from northeast in the Northern Hemisphere and southeast in Southern Hemisphere. Sailors carrying goods from Africa to

The Windy City

Winds take some pretty strange turns in cities. Coming down narrow city streets, winds bounce off buildings and whirl in different directions. Blowing around and over buildings, winds become very strong. Chicago, Illinois, is often called the Windy City because of its famous windy weather. Strong winds blowing off nearby Lake Michigan are magnified by the buildings. In some places on Chicago's Michigan Avenue, handrails in the street help people walk against the strong winds coming off buildings.

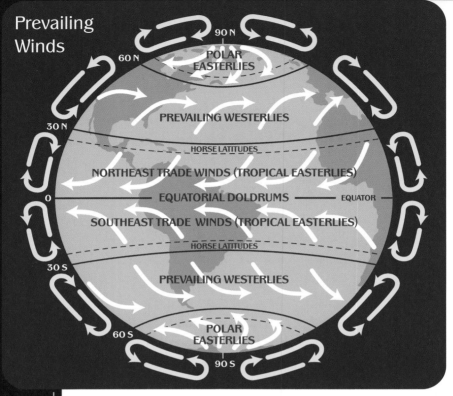

Prevailing
Winds

90 N

POLAR EASTERLIES

60 N

PREVAILING WESTERLIES

30 N

HORSE LATITUDES

NORTHEAST TRADE WINDS (TROPICAL EASTERLIES)

0 — EQUATORIAL DOLDRUMS — EQUATOR —

SOUTHEAST TRADE WINDS (TROPICAL EASTERLIES)

HORSE LATITUDES

30 S

PREVAILING WESTERLIES

60 S

POLAR EASTERLIES

90 S

Prevailing winds, named for the direction from which they come, flow around Earth in wide bands. They are called prevailing winds because they almost always flow in the same direction.

South or Central America depended on the trade winds because their course was so regular. Between the trade winds, around the equator, there is a belt of rising air that is usually mild and calm. This region is called the doldrums. Early sailing ships that traveled in the doldrums could be stranded for weeks with no winds.

At about 30 degrees north and south latitude (the measure of the distance from the equator toward the poles, expressed in degrees of a circle along the curved surface of Earth), the rising warm air from the equator has cooled enough to sink rapidly. Warm air masses are then drawn toward the colder North and South Poles and form the prevailing westerlies. Most of the United States, Europe, and Asia fall within the belt of prevailing westerly winds. Old-time sailing ships used them for the return voyage from the Americas to Europe. The boundaries between the trade winds and the prevailing westerlies are usually areas of nearly still air. They are called the horse latitudes because ships were sometimes stranded for weeks and had to get rid of excess cargo, which sometimes included horses.

Close to the poles, where Earth receives the least direct rays of the sun, it is warmed less than the rest of the globe. Warm air flowing toward the poles rises, and cold air from the polar regions moves down to replace it. This creates the third pair of wind belts, the polar easterlies. These winds are usually weaker than the westerlies in the middle latitudes because the temperature differences are smaller.

The Jet Streams

High up in the atmosphere, where the edges of two wind belts meet, warm air and cold air come into contact. As usual, when this happens, winds are created. Until the 1940s, no one was aware there were winds at the tropopause—the boundary between the troposphere and the stratosphere—5 to 8 miles (8 to 13 km) above the surface. In World War II (1939–1945), American planes on a bombing mission to Tokyo, Japan, climbed to an altitude of 30,000 feet (about 5.7 miles—more than 9 km) to avoid the Japanese antiaircraft fire. Suddenly the fliers found their planes zooming along at 450 miles (724 km) per hour, far faster than any plane had ever flown before. They had picked up a tailwind that was blowing more than 150 miles (241 km) per hour. In later years, it was found that just as there are prevailing winds in the lower atmosphere, winds also follow regular paths up in the tropopause. These winds were named jet streams, and their paths were mapped.

The jet streams generally blow around Earth from west to east, but their paths are not straight. They curve and zigzag like the body of a snake wriggling along, bending north or south to flow around warm or cool air masses. The polar jet streams, wandering between the polar easterlies and the prevailing westerlies, meet many high- and low-pressure systems along their winding paths. The subtropical jet streams, located where the trade wind belts meet the prevailing westerlies, have a straighter path. The paths of the jet streams also differ according to the season, lying closer to the equator in the winter and closer to the poles in the summer. The eastward path of the jet streams tends to move storms from west to east. During the summer in the Northern Hemisphere, though, a reverse jet stream blows from east to west over the Indian Ocean and Africa. The reason is that the vast lands of Asia absorb so much heat from the sun that the air above them grows even warmer than air at the equator!

Wind Force

In 1805 the British admiral Sir Francis Beaufort created the Beaufort wind scale to indicate wind speeds. The stronger a wind is, the faster it blows. Beaufort assigned numbers to different forces of wind to indicate their strength.

Beaufort Number	Wind Name	Miles per Hour (km per hour)	Effect on Land
0	Calm	less than 1 (less than 2)	Calm—no motion
1	Light air	1-3 (2-5)	Chimney smoke drifts
2	Light breeze	4-7 (6-11)	Leaves rustle
3	Gentle breeze	8-12 (13-19)	Small twigs move
4	Moderate breeze	13-18 (21-29)	Small branches sway
5	Fresh breeze	19-24 (31-39)	Small trees sway
6	Strong breeze	25-31 (40-50)	Large branches sway
7	Moderate gale*	32-38 (52-61)	Whole trees sway
8	Fresh gale	39-46 (63-74)	Tree branches snap
9	Strong gale	47-54 (76-87)	Minor damage to buildings
10	Whole gale	55-63 (89-101)	Trees uprooted
11	Storm	64-74 (103-119)	Widespread damage
12	Hurricane	75+ (121+)	Houses blown down; major damage

* Gale means "windstorm"

chapter four

Clouds and Weather

It's fun to look at the clouds in the sky and pick out a dog, an elephant, or a giraffe. Clouds come in all sorts of shapes and sizes, which makes it easy to imagine that they take on the form of an animal or some other object. It is hard to imagine, however, that although clouds look thick and solid, they are actually made up of billions of tiny water droplets or ice crystals.

What Are Clouds?

Clouds form from moisture in the air. This moisture is water vapor, the invisible gas form of water. The process starts when an area is heated by the sun, creating a large bubble of warm air. The bubble rises like a hot-air balloon. As it floats upward, the bubble may then pass through a wind of cooler air. The air bubble cools and can hold less water vapor. The bubble reaches its dew point when the air has become so cold that the water vapor condenses onto dust particles. The invisible gas bubble then turns into visible droplets of water (dew) or even ice crystals.

Clouds come in all shapes and sizes. Just a few examples of the different looks of clouds are cumulus clouds (top left), *cirrus clouds* (top right), *and altocumulus clouds* (right).

You have probably seen dew droplets on plant leaves or blades of grass early on a spring morning. If the temperature is cold enough, the dew point is not reached until the freezing temperature, at 32°F (0°C), which turns the dew

These leaves are covered with frost, which formed after the dew point reached the freezing temperature.

into frozen water vapor called frost.

Clouds get their different shapes from the way the water droplets and ice crystals form. Clouds stop rising into the air when the bubble is too cold and heavy to go any higher.

Clouds are an important part of weather because forms of precipitation—which include rain, snow, sleet, and hail—develop inside them. Precipitation is moisture that condenses in the atmosphere and falls to the ground. All clouds contain water droplets or ice crystals. As the clouds rise higher into colder air, more water vapor condenses, forming tiny drops of water. Soon the water droplets join with others and eventually become so heavy that they fall from the clouds as rain. It takes about a million cloud droplets to form an average raindrop. When raindrops fall through a band of cold air on the way down, they turn into tiny balls of ice. These may precipitate in the form of sleet (a mixture of liquid and frozen rain), or they may grow into larger balls of ice called hailstones. When the cloud reaches freezing temperatures, the water droplets become ice crystals. They join together to form snowflakes. These snowflakes usually fall down

Every snowflake is made up of tiny water droplets that become ice crystals. They join together to form a snowflake.

An Amazing Discovery

American scientist Wilson A. Bentley loved snowflakes so much that he drew pictures and took photographs of them. In 1880 he examined a snowflake under a microscope so he could see what it really looked like up close. Bentley thought he'd see just a piece of ice, but instead, it had a delicate hexagonal—six-sided—shape made of ice crystals. He used his camera to take a picture of the snowflake through the microscope. In all his observations, Bentley never found two snowflakes exactly alike. Scientists believe that identical snowflakes could exist but that this is very unlikely because such huge numbers of tiny ice crystals combine to form each one.

onto Earth's surface in clusters of hundreds of flakes and blanket the ground in what we call snow.

Ground Clouds

Have you ever walked through fog? Fog is actually a cloud that touches the ground. The only difference between clouds and fog is the way they are formed. Clouds form when warm, moist air rises and then cools. Fog forms when air cools near the ground. This usually happens at night.

Fog may feel damper than normal air, and it is difficult to see through, especially at night. When

The Golden Gate Bridge becomes almost invisible in a fog cloud. The bridge in California connects the city of San Francisco (on the Pacific Ocean) to Marin County and is often wrapped in fog. This happens because the warm California air is cooled by the cold ocean currents.

people drive at night, the light from their headlights hits the water droplets in the fog, which act like tiny mirrors, bouncing the light back into their eyes. The fog then looks like a solid wall of bright light. Drivers should always use their low beams in foggy weather. High beams only make the wall of bright light brighter.

In certain cities, fog may turn into pollutant-filled smog. This condition occurs when a layer of warm air settles over a land area that is enclosed within a valley, such as Los Angeles, California. Normally, warm air rises, taking away dust particles and pollutants from the city below. But if these pollutants are stopped by the blanket of warm air, the dust and chemicals are trapped

Did You Know?

Two cities that are famous for their frequent fogs are San Francisco, California, and London, England. The thick fogs in London are often called pea-soupers.

Make Your Own Cloud

When you go outside on a cold winter day, you can usually see your breath. This happens in the same way that clouds and fog are formed in the air. The air in your breath is warm. When you breathe out, this warm air rises and meets with the cold outside air. The water vapor in your breath then condenses and turns into a puff of cloud, filled with tiny droplets of water.

at lower levels of the atmosphere. Pollution-control regulations in Los Angeles are especially strict to try to reduce smog.

Smog is often a problem in Los Angeles, California. The city has reduced its smog problems in recent years. But it is still ranked as the most polluted city in the United States, according to the American Lung Association.

Fog That's Not Foggy

A strange kind of fog known as the *garúa* sometimes forms in areas along the coast of Peru and northern Chile, in South America. This fog is not cloudy—it's clear—but so wet that drivers need to use their windshield wipers. The garúa starts out as normal fog, formed when the warm air above the nearby Pacific Ocean passes over the cold Humboldt Current. When ocean breezes carry the fog into the hot, dry air over the land, water droplets in the fog begin to evaporate. The droplets shrink into extremely small particles, producing a nearly invisible but very wet fog.

Cloud Classification

In 1803 British scientist Luke Howard suggested a simple system for identifying cloud formations. He classified clouds into three main types according to their shape and the height where they form. *Cirrus* is from the Latin word meaning "hairlike" or "curly." *Cumulus* is from the Latin word meaning "heap" or "pile." And *stratus* is from the Latin word meaning "layered." For clouds that seemed to be a mixture of more than one type, Howard combined the names— for example, *cirrostratus.* He also added the term nimbus to describe clouds that produce rain or snow and added the prefix *alto,* meaning "high," to distinguish a cloud at a higher altitude from a lower cloud of the same type.

Did You Know?

Cirrus clouds are often called mare's tails because strong winds blow them into wispy curls, like the hairs in a horse's tail.

Three main kinds of clouds are found at the highest levels, about 3 to 5 miles (5 to 8 km) above Earth's surface: cirrus, cirrocumulus, and cirrostratus. Cirrus clouds are thin, white feathery clouds made of only ice crystals because of cold temperatures so high up. Cirrus clouds that form patchy clumps are called cirrocumulus. Cirrus clouds that form thin, white sheets that blanket the sky are called cirrostratus. They may spread out over hundreds of miles.

Medium-level clouds, about 1.2 to 4.3 miles (1.9 to 6.9 km) above Earth's surface, include altocumulus, altostratus, and nimbostratus. Altocumulus clouds are shaped like round heaps.

Types of Clouds

cirrostratus · cirrus · cirrocumulus · cumulonimbus · altocumulus · altostratus · cumulus · stratocumulus · stratus · nimbocumulus

km: 9 · 6 · 3 · 0

miles: 5.6 · 3.7 · 1.8 · 0

These are the main types of clouds. Their shapes and altitudes give clues to what kind of weather is coming.

They may also appear in patches or rows. Altostratus clouds are thin sheets of clouds that cover the sky. Nimbostratus clouds are thick, dark clouds that usually bring rain or snow. They can sometimes be found closer to the ground.

Clouds at the lowest levels, from Earth's surface to about 1.2 miles (1.9 km), include stratus clouds and cumulus clouds. Stratus clouds look like smooth, thin sheets. Cumulus clouds look like heaps of fluffy cotton balls. Stratocumulus clouds are rounded clouds that look as if they are joined together to form a low sheet that covers the sky. Cumulonimbus clouds are dark cumulus clouds that can stretch high into the sky. They are commonly called thunderheads because they often bring thunderstorms.

Weather forecasters can tell if we will have good or bad weather by studying the clouds. Some general rules can be fairly reliable predictors. For instance, the higher the cloud, the nicer the weather. Lower clouds contain more moisture, which weighs them down. Moisture-soaked storm clouds also typically look gray. (The extra water particles block the sun's rays.) The more moisture in a cloud, the darker it looks and the more likely it will produce precipitation.

Cloudy Forecasting

The kinds of clouds in the sky can help you guess what your weather will be like.

Cirrus clouds: A few cirrus clouds scattered high in the sky are a sign of good weather. When cirrus clouds look like long, wavy strands of mare's tails, rain may be coming.

Cumulus clouds: Fluffy white cumulus clouds that look like cotton balls are usually signs of good weather. But on hot, humid summer days, these cumulus clouds spread out and rise higher in the sky. Then they turn into cumulonimbus clouds, which can bring a thunderstorm.

Stratus clouds: Stratus clouds close together, covering much of the sky, form a pattern like the scales of a fish. This is called a mackerel sky and is a sign that rain is coming.

chapter five

Our World's Climates

Many scientists believe that the first humans lived in Africa, near the equator. Under such warm conditions, early humans did not need clothes or shelter, and food grew all year long. Gradually, people started to spread out into areas with cooler temperatures. They learned how to make tools and discovered how to use and control fire. They were able to tolerate colder weather because they could build fires and shelters and use animal skins as clothing.

For thousands of years, humans have been adapting to different types of weather conditions throughout the world. There are so many to choose from! Can you imagine living in an area where there are no seasons? Around the North and South Poles, the weather is cold throughout the year. Near the equator, except in high mountain areas, the weather is always warm. But at the middle latitudes, there are seasons. In most places in this belt, the winters are cold and the summers are hot. Every place on Earth, no matter where it is or how small it is, has its own climate.

What Is Climate?

Climate is the overall pattern of weather conditions in a particular place. Climatologists, or scientists who study climate, find out the climate of a region by studying it over a period of years. Climate is determined according to average monthly and yearly temperatures and amounts of precipitation. Climatologists also consider how seasons vary throughout the year. Both Saint Louis, Missouri, and San Francisco, California, have an average yearly temperature of 55°F (13°C). But these two cities have different climates. Saint Louis has rather cold winters and hot summers. San Francisco, however, has fairly mild, rainy winters, and cool, almost rainless, summers with frequent fog.

Saint Louis, Missouri, and San Francisco, California, have the same average yearly temperature. But the weather in Saint Louis (below left) *was sunny and hot at nearly 100°F (38°C) in July 2006. In San Francisco* (below right), *the temperature was 67°F (19°C) with gray skies and drizzle during the same July week.*

Seasons of Change

Why does the weather change during certain times of the year? Seasons occur because some parts of Earth receive more of the sun's rays than others. Earth rotates once every twenty-four hours on an axis that is a bit tilted. (Earth's axis is an imaginary line passing through the globe from the North Pole to the South Pole.) Places near the pole tilted away from the sun receive the sun's rays less directly, while those at the

The changing seasons are due to the tilt of Earth's axis as it orbits the sun. In summer, the part of the globe tilted toward the sun gets more sunlight, and the days are longer than in the winter. In spring and fall, the days are of equal length, and sunlight is spread out equally from the North Pole to the South Pole.

The Earth's Seasons

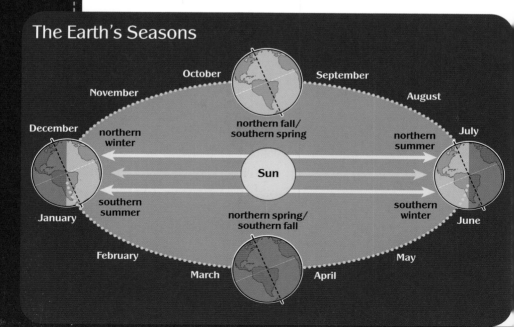

other pole get more sunlight. But Earth also revolves around the sun, taking about 365 days to travel all the way around the oval path called its orbit. The pole that is tilted toward the sun at one side of its orbit is tilted away from the sun when Earth is at the opposite side, half a year later. During the year, the seasons change depending on the amount of sunlight that hits each part of the world. Places in the Northern and Southern Hemispheres have their seasons at opposite times of the year. When the Northern Hemisphere has winter, the Southern Hemisphere has summer.

Did You Know?

We have day and night because Earth rotates. The part of Earth facing the sun has daytime. The part facing away from the sun has nighttime. It takes twenty-four hours for Earth to make a complete turn. The amounts of daylight and darkness change with the seasons because Earth is tilted on its axis.

As people began to move into the temperate latitudes, they had to learn to store food to eat over the cold winters, when no plants were growing. Now that goods can be shipped from one part of the world to another, we can eat foods out of season. Supermarkets in North America, for example, stock summer fruits and vegetables all year round. The ones on sale in the winter are imported from places in the Southern Hemisphere, such as Chile or Australia, where it is summer.

Some places have only two seasons. In the Arctic (North Pole) and Antarctic (South Pole) regions, a few months of summer warmth are followed by a long, cold winter. In some places near the equator, there are also only two seasons: a hot, dry season and a wet season. But most parts of our planet have four seasons: summer, fall, winter, and spring.

In the Northern Hemisphere, summer begins on June 20 or 21, the summer solstice, when the sun reaches its highest point in the sky. There are more hours of daylight than on any other day, making it the

This photo was taken shortly after midnight in May 2003 at the base camp at Denali National Park and Reserve in Alaska. It shows that there is no true darkness a month before the summer solstice in the Northern Hemisphere.

The changing of the color of leaves, such as these in Massachusetts, from green to brown, gold, orange, and red, happens every autumn.

longest day of the year. As you get closer to the North Pole, the sun doesn't set at all for longer periods around the solstice.

Autumn, or fall, begins on September 22 or 23, the autumnal equinox. At this time, the sun appears to be directly above the equator. There are twelve hours of daylight and twelve hours of darkness all over the earth, except near the poles.

Winter starts on December 21 or 22, the winter solstice. The sun reaches the lowest point in the sky, and there are fewer hours of daylight than on any other date, making it the shortest day of the year. In the extreme north, there is total darkness for weeks.

Spring begins on March 20 or 21, the vernal equinox. As on the autumnal equinox, the sun is just above the equator and there are twelve hours of daylight and twelve hours of darkness.

In the Southern Hemisphere, the solstices and equinoxes occur on the same dates, but the seasons (spring, fall, winter, summer) are the reverse of those in the Northern Hemisphere.

Types of Climates

There is a wide range of climates all over the world. Although climates can vary a great deal from one place to another, there are four main climate zones on Earth: polar, temperate, tropical, and subtropical.

World Record Weather

Highest temperature: In al-Aziziyah, Libya, record temperatures reached 136°F (58°C) on September 13, 1922. (In North America, 134°F (57°C) was recorded in Death Valley, California on July 10, 1918.)

Lowest temperature: In Vostok, Antarctica, temperatures dropped to -129°F (-89°C) on July 21, 1983. (In North America, -81°F (-63°C) was recorded in Snag, Canada, on February 3, 1947.)

Strongest winds: In Mount Washington, New Hampshire, on April 12, 1934, a gust of wind reached 231 miles (372 km) per hour.

The polar zones, which include the North and South Poles, are the coldest regions on Earth. The poles are covered by large, dry, cold air masses. In the Antarctic, temperatures can fall to as low as $-129°F$ ($-89°C$) in the winter. Most of the Antarctic regions are covered with thick ice all year round. The land areas in the Arctic are also very cold, but in the summer, snow melts and plants can grow for the animals to eat.

The temperate zones are regions that have relatively warm summers, cold winters, and rain and snow. These regions are strongly influenced by wind and ocean currents, which bring a

Driest region: In Arica, Chile, the average annual rainfall is .03 inch (.08 cm).

Heaviest rainfall: In Cherrapunji, India, a record 1,041.8 inches (2,646 cm) of rain fell between August 1860 and July 1861.

Heaviest snowfall: Rainier Paradise Ranger Station in Washington recorded 1,122 inches (2,850 cm) of snow during the 1971-1972 winter season, the record for North America.

Largest hailstone: A hailstone that measured 17.5 inches (45 cm) around the surface and weighed about 1.7 pounds (0.8 kg) fell in Coffeyville, Kansas, on September 3, 1970.

lot of weather variation. Much of the United States and Europe has temperate climates.

The tropical zones are regions that are close to the equator. The climate is usually hot and wet throughout the year in most tropical areas. In some areas of the tropics, such as parts of South America and Africa, there are separate wet and dry seasons.

The subtropical zones are the regions just north and south of the tropical zones. These areas have warm temperatures for most of the year, and winter

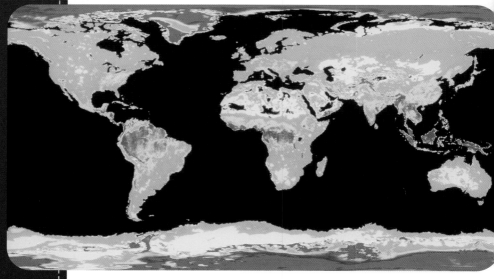

This satellite radar image showing a flattened-out map of Earth is colored to indicate Earth's climate regions. Arctic and Antarctic ice is magenta. Tropical rain forests in Africa, South America, and the islands between Asia and Australia are deep blue. Deserts are yellow with darker areas.

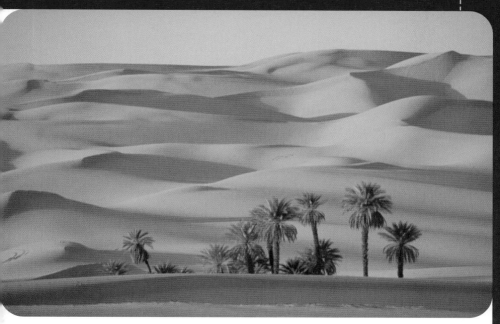

Very few plants can grow in the dry Sahara in northern Africa. These palms manage to survive in the dry heat near an oasis, a place where underground water comes near the surface.

temperatures rarely fall below freezing. Some subtropical areas (including Florida) are rainy, and others (including the Sahara in northern Africa) are very dry. Deserts, such as the Sahara, are dry regions that get very little rain, so they have very few plants and animals.

Stormy Weather

For centuries people have been amazed and confused by the mysteries of nature. Before the scientific measurement of weather, they had many different ideas to explain strange weather conditions. For instance, some Native Americans believed that the sacred thunderbird created thunder during storms as it flapped its tremendous wings and flashed lightning from its beak. Some ancient Greeks and Romans, on the other hand, were convinced that angry gods were hurling thunderbolts from the heavens.

We are still rather amazed and sometimes confused about the mysteries of nature. But we do know that storms are caused by the movements of cold and warm air masses, which are constantly swirling around in the atmosphere. When these air masses mix, the results may be violent. Storms can bring not only strong winds and precipitation but also sudden discharges of electricity, producing the crackle and roar of lightning and thunder.

The buildup of cumulonimbus clouds, or thunderheads (left), *usually means that a storm with lightning* (right) *and thunder is on the way.*

Thunderstorms

Thunderstorms are the most common type of weather storm. There are as many as sixteen million each year—up to fifty thousand a day! In North America, most thunderstorms take place in the spring and summer. Tall, puffy cumulonimbus clouds are clues that a thunderstorm is coming, giving them the nickname thunderheads. These clouds need more moisture and heat to form than others, which is why they usually occur during warm weather. During hot, humid weather, thunderheads may get very tall, sometimes reaching an altitude of 60,000 feet (more than 11 miles, or 18 km) or higher, where the temperatures are below freezing.

The winds inside a storm cloud swirl up and down at fast speeds. This makes the water vapor in the air condense very quickly, producing heavy rainfalls. These moving air currents also cause the water droplets and ice crystals to break apart and crash into one another. This violent activity produces a charge of static electricity—the way rubbing your feet on a rug does. Some particles pick up electrons when they collide, gaining a negative electrical charge.

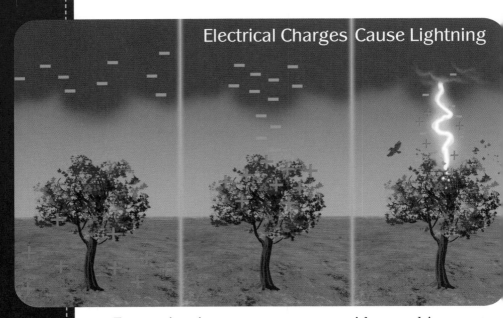

Electrical Charges Cause Lightning

Fast-moving air currents cause water particles to crash into each other. They pick up or lose electrons and become electrically charged. When the charge builds up, the electrons move down toward the ground in the form of a sudden bolt of lightning.

Other particles lose electrons, becoming positively charged. The positively charged particles tend to cluster in the upper part of a cloud and the negative ones in the lower part. Particles in the land below the cloud are also affected by these electrical charges. Positive charges build up at the surface, especially at the tops of tall buildings, trees, and other objects that are closest to the clouds.

Air molecules are normally good insulators—they do not conduct electricity—and keep the positive and negative particles separated. But when the electricity stored in a storm cloud builds up enough, the insulation breaks down. Then electrons move from negative to positive particles—an electric current suddenly flows in the form of a bolt of lightning. Lightning may flash within a cloud, between layers with opposite electrical charges. It may also arc between two clouds, and it can strike downward to electrically charged objects on the ground below. The flow of electricity in a lightning bolt is enormously powerful, heating up the surrounding air molecules to as much as 50,000°F (nearly 28,000°C). The heated air explodes outward, producing the rumbling roar of thunder. We see the lightning before we hear the thunder because light travels faster

> ## Did You Know?
> The old saying "Lightning never strikes twice in the same place" is completely false. In fact, the Empire State Building in New York City has been struck by lightning a dozen times in a single storm and as many as five hundred times each year.

than sound. You can tell how far away the lightning is by counting the seconds between the lightning flash and the rumbling thunder. Each five seconds you count means about 1 mile (1.6 km) of distance.

Thunderstorms can also bring some serious flooding problems. For instance, moist winds blowing over the Indian Ocean bring heavy rains to India and Bangladesh during the monsoon season. Monsoon rains begin in the summer and last for six months. Monsoons are helpful for the crops but often cause serious flooding problems and significant damage.

Commuters in Dhaka, Bangladesh, make their way through flooded streets in July 2005. Monsoon season often brings flooding to Bangladesh and neighboring India.

Hailstorms sometimes occur during thunderstorms. We know that the air currents in a thundercloud rise and fall constantly. As water droplets are carried up into the freezing temperatures at high altitudes, they

These golf ball-sized hailstones fell in Kansas.

freeze into tiny ice crystals. Then they fall and are swept up again by rising air currents. A layer of ice is added to the frozen droplet each time it reaches the freezing temperatures, producing a larger and larger ball of ice—a hailstone. Eventually it gets so heavy that it falls from the cloud. Hailstones can be dangerous to cars, houses, crops, and people. In some areas, hailstones have been as big as golf balls.

Tornadoes

Tornadoes, also called twisters or cyclones, are extremely violent weather storms. Although they occur in many regions all over the world, most of them happen in the United States. In the Central States, in particular, a combination of flatlands and wind patterns allows cold air masses from the Arctic to collide violently with warm air from the Gulf of Mexico. In Europe and Asia, mountain ranges keep the very cold and very warm air masses from colliding.

> ### Did You Know?
> People who've heard one say that a tornado sounds like dozens of roaring express trains.

This tornado touched down in Kansas in June 2005. The funnel cloud moved across an interstate highway, overturning semi-trucks along the way.

Experiment: Make Your Own Cyclone

You can make a model of a tornado. You need two soft-drink bottles, water, and a roll of duct tape. Fill one bottle with water. Place the empty bottle upside down on top of the water-filled one so that the two openings are together. Tape the necks of the bottles together tightly. Turn the two bottles upside down so that the liquid is in the top bottle. Swirl the liquid for a few seconds, and then watch what happens. (Note that your model tornado is made of water. A real twister is formed from air masses.)

Tornadoes are low-pressure systems created in thunderclouds. Sometimes fast-rising air currents in the cloud cause the warm and cold air masses to mix together, and they begin to spin. This funnel of spinning air, a tornado, drops from the storm cloud. Sometimes its tip touches the ground.

Tornadoes produce the most powerful winds on Earth, whirling as fast as 250 miles (400 km) per hour. The low-pressure area at the center of the funnel produces a powerful upward draft. As the bottom of the tornado touches the ground, it will suck up anything in its path like a powerful vacuum cleaner. A tornado can lift large trees out of the ground and pick up a car and throw it hundreds of feet away. Tornadoes are so unpredictable that they can destroy a few houses on a street while leaving the rest untouched. Tornadoes have also been known to lift things into the air and then set them down without a scratch. Tornadoes usually last for only fifteen minutes but can cause tremendous damage.

Hurricanes

Hurricanes are the deadliest storms on Earth. They kill more people every year than all other storms combined. Called typhoons in the western Pacific, they are violent windstorms that form in tropical regions and cover hundreds of miles. Hurricane winds can blow from 74 to 200 miles (119 to 322 km) per hour.

Hurricanes start off as small thunderstorms over warm, tropical oceans. Warm, moist air rises into the atmosphere, creating an area of low air pressure. As air is sucked in from the surrounding area to replace the rising air, it creates a

This satellite image of Hurricane Katrina shows the storm bearing down on Louisiana and Mississippi in August 2005.

whirlpool of hot, moist air that spirals around a center filled with low-pressure, calm air, called the eye. The eye of the hurricane is sunny, with a blue sky, and no wind. To observers on the ground, the storm appears to be over. But then, as the hurricane continues to travel, the eye passes over and the winds start blowing just as violently as before. Soon after it forms, the hurricane may move from the ocean waters onto land, bringing heavy rains. Because a hurricane draws its energy from warm water, the storm gradually becomes weaker once it reaches land. But before it is over, it can do tremendous damage—uprooting trees, tossing cars and other heavy objects, destroying houses, flooding roads, and killing people.

Winter Storms

Blizzards are severe snowstorms with strong, cold winds that blow at least 35 miles (56 km) per hour or more. The blowing snow greatly reduces visibility (creating a whiteout) and can produce huge snowdrifts.

The freezing temperatures and blowing snow of a blizzard can cripple a whole city, producing power outages and bad driving conditions. Heavy snowfalls can be extremely dangerous in the mountains. When spring arrives, the snow on the mountainsides starts to melt. This loosens up the packed snow and ice, which may cause an avalanche. Tons of snow and ice come crashing down the mountain, burying everything in their path.

Did You Know?
It can be too cold to snow. Remember: Cold air cannot hold as much water vapor as warm air. If it is too cold, there is not enough water vapor in the air to produce precipitation. Snow usually occurs when the temperature is close to the freezing point.

Drivers make their way slowly through the falling snow on a Colorado highway. The state received two major winter storms just days apart in late December 2006.

chapter seven

Our Changing Climate

Scientists have pieced together a record of Earth's climate for the past 600 million years of its 4.6-billion-year history. Rock formations, fossils, and other bits of evidence have revealed that Earth's climate has gone through some major changes.

For instance, a tree grows a new ring for each year it lives. A study of its rings can not only show how old the tree is, but their thickness may indicate the climate when they were formed. For example, thin rings may be a sign of poor growth due to droughts or severe springs frosts.

Scientists have also collected animal fossils found deep in the ocean floor. These specimens provide information about the temperatures of the oceans about 100 million years ago.

The Ice Ages

Throughout Earth's history, the climate has alternated between periods of warm weather and periods of cold weather. The ice ages mark the most dramatic changes in Earth's climate. During an ice age, large sheets of ice, called glaciers, advanced from the polar regions to cover more of Earth's surface.

This glacier in the Salvesen Mountains in Antarctica is melting at a rapid pace. Since the 1980s, global warming has hastened the melting of glaciers around the world.

Scientists believe that we have had several ice ages, some more significant than others. The last ice age ended about ten thousand years ago. At its peak, about eighteen thousand years ago, glaciers covered all of Canada, much of the United States, and most of northwestern Europe, with ice hundreds and even thousands of feet thick. Glaciers often carried large rocks, which were left behind when the ice melted. Glaciers have changed the surface of mountains. One side may be smooth and rounded, while the other may be rough, with a steep slope.

Did You Know?

Plants and plantlike organisms in the world's oceans account for about two-thirds of the photosynthesis that occurs on Earth. Like land plants, the photosynthetic organisms in the water also absorb carbon dioxide during this process. However, when pollutants are dumped into the waters, some of the organisms die. This reduces another good way of eliminating the excess carbon dioxide in the air.

Since the last ice age, Earth has been on a warming trend called an interglacial period. The only remains of the once great glaciers are the ice sheets in the polar regions that cover Antarctica and most of Greenland. However, people recorded a period of cold climate between 1550 and 1850, known as the Little Ice Age.

In 1920 Serbian mathematician Milutin Milankovitch provided a theory that explained why ice ages come and go. He claimed that Earth's climate is determined by how much energy it receives from the sun. Milankovitch explained that Earth's orbit, rotation, and tilt on its axis go through changes according to fairly regular cycles with periods of 20,000, 40,000, and 100,000 years. The interaction of these cycles results in a change in the seasonal cycles, which periodically reduces the amount of solar energy that reaches Earth. According to this theory, we can expect another ice age in the future—the glaciers will return in about 50,000 to 70,000 years.

The Greenhouse Effect

Since 1850, when the Little Ice Age ended, climates around the world have been on a warming trend. Normally, only a small amount of the sun's energy reaches Earth. The rest of it is reflected (bounced) back into space by clouds or by snow and ice at the polar regions. Our planet stays warm because gases in the atmosphere, such as carbon dioxide, trap heat, just

Gases in the atmosphere, such as carbon dioxide, trap and hold some of the heat from sunlight, like the glass walls of a greenhouse. In recent decades, human activities have produced more of these greenhouse gases. As a result, Earth's average temperature has been rising.

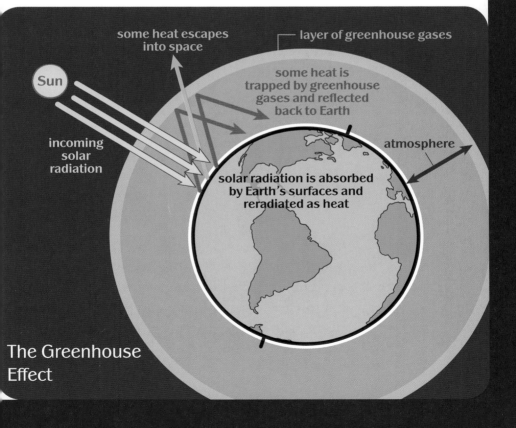

some heat escapes into space

layer of greenhouse gases

Sun

some heat is trapped by greenhouse gases and reflected back to Earth

incoming solar radiation

atmosphere

solar radiation is absorbed by Earth's surfaces and reradiated as heat

The Greenhouse Effect

like the glass in a greenhouse that allows plants to grow even in the winter. Scientists call this warming of Earth the greenhouse effect.

Since the mid-nineteenth century, human settlement and industrialization have had a serious impact on our weather and climate. People have burned fossil fuels—coal, oil, and gas—to provide

Global Warming Today

Scientists have been warning the public about global warming for many years. But it wasn't until 2006 that it gained worldwide attention when the documentary film, *An Inconvenient Truth*, came out. The film, featuring former U.S. vice president Al Gore, later won an Oscar. Gore discusses scientific evidence for global warming and the role that humans play in adding to the warming of the planet. Global warming, he insists, has already had serious effects on our weather and climate. If we do not reduce the billions of tons of carbon dioxide we produce every year, the effects could be disastrous. Here's what we know about global warming:

- The levels of carbon dioxide in the atmosphere have increased by 35 percent since the start of the Industrial Revolution in the mid-1800s.

energy for their factories, buildings, homes, and vehicles. When these fuels are burned, carbon dioxide and other waste products are released into the atmosphere, producing most of the air pollution in our environment. Normally, carbon dioxide, released from rocks and produced by the respiration (breathing) of living things, is present in the atmosphere in small amounts—just enough to keep our world comfortably warm.

- The average global temperature increased 1°F (0.6°C) during the twentieth century. If carbon dioxide and other greenhouse gases are not reduced in the near future, Earth's average temperature could rise an additional 3° to 9°F (1.7° to 5°C) over the next hundred years.
- Nineteen out of the twenty hottest years on record occurred between 1980 and 2005.
- Glaciers are melting.
- Sea levels have already risen 4 to 8 inches (10 to 20 cm) in the past century.
- At least 279 species of plants and animals are already having problems adapting to the warming temperatures. Many animals have moved to colder regions.
- The number of severe storms, droughts, and wildfires has increased. (The number of hurricanes has almost doubled since the 1980s.)

Cars produce carbon dioxide when they burn gasoline. So this New York City traffic jam is adding to the global warming effects of greenhouse gases.

The burning of fuels, however, has been increasing the amount of carbon dioxide in the atmosphere. It's kind of like putting an extra blanket on your bed; the extra carbon dioxide blanket has been making the earth warmer. And warmer temperatures mean serious problems for our planet.

Many scientists believe that the increasing levels of carbon dioxide and other heat-trapping gases in the atmosphere have led to a global warming—a significant rise in the average temperature throughout the world. Signs point to a global warming over the last century. Over the next hundred years, global warming could increase Earth's average temperature by a few degrees. This does not sound like much, but it would be enough to melt part of the ice and snow in the polar regions. There would be some good effects—an increase in the amount of land that could be used for farming, for example. In fact, at one time, Russian scientists proposed a massive project to melt the polar ice.

Other effects, however, could be disastrous. The melted ice would raise the sea level and flood many of the world's coastal areas, such as New York City and the whole state of Florida.

Plant a Tree!

Do you know what you can do to lower the levels of carbon dioxide in the atmosphere? Plant a tree! During photosynthesis, plants absorb far more carbon dioxide than they use for respiration. That is one big reason why we need to save the rain forests. When people cut down trees, they reduce the amount of plant life that can soak up carbon dioxide.

Volcanoes and Weather

In June 1991, Mount Pinatubo, a volcano in the Philippines, erupted after being inactive for more than six hundred years. Loads of ash and debris were thrown up into Earth's atmosphere, changing weather patterns all over the world in 1992. This happened because particulates (soot, ash, and other substances) in the atmosphere block the sun's rays, making the weather cooler than usual. The extra particles in the air may also cause large amounts of water vapor to condense, producing heavy rain or snowfall. While many scientists believe that we are seeing a global warming, events such as volcanic eruptions can put a temporary halt to the world's warming trend.

The Arrival of El Niño

Every three to seven years, a warm ocean current called El Niño arrives off the Pacific Coast of South America, causing some serious changes in the usual weather patterns all over the world. El Niño is short for El Niño de Navidad, Spanish for "Christ child," so-named because it appears around Christmastime. There is a change in the direction of winds and ocean currents, which makes for unusually warm waters in the southeastern tropical Pacific Ocean.

Normally, the warm waters remain in the western tropical Pacific, where the temperatures are 18°F (10°C) warmer than in the eastern waters near the coasts of Peru and Ecuador. In the western Pacific, the air pressure is low. Warm air rises, forming clouds and resulting in heavy rainfalls in southeastern Asia, New Guinea, and northern Australia. In the eastern Pacific, the waters are much colder and the air pressure is high, creating a fairly dry climate along the South American coast. Trade winds usually blow from east to west, moving the warm surface waters toward the west and leaving cold water at the surface in the east.

When El Niño arrives, however, the easterly trade winds weaken or even reverse, blowing winds from west to east. As a result, the warm water in the western Pacific flows back toward the east, and the surface temperatures along the South American coast become warmer. Therefore, the wet weather that normally occurs in the western Pacific moves toward the east, and the dry weather that is typical for the eastern Pacific shifts over to the west. During El Niño, heavy rains fall in South America, and Asia, India, and southern Africa have very dry weather. El Niño can also cause unusual weather in large areas of the United States.

The effects of El Niño are often disastrous. Its appearance in the 1997–1998 winter season is believed to have been the El Niño of the century. It brought one of the most powerful storms on record to California. The state was flooded with heavy rains, strong winds, and 30-foot (9 m) waves along the coast. Floodwaters destroyed railroads and highways, demolished hundreds of homes, and caused the loss of lives. At the same time, other strange weather events affected different parts of the United States. In Florida a huge storm set off

Waves pound the pilings of oceanfront homes during an El Niño-powered storm in southern California in December 1997.

destructive tornadoes that tore up neighborhoods and killed more than forty people. In Ohio, heavy snowfalls covered parts of the state. However, large areas of the eastern and north-central United States had the warmest winter in years, with an early blossoming of plants.

Changing Weather, Changing Landscape

Our world's weather has been changing for millions of years. Year after year, the sun shines; the rain pours; the snow and ice pile up; the fierce winds blow; and the ocean waters crash against rocks. These weather events are continually changing Earth's landscape in a gradual process called weathering. Weathering occurs in various forms.

Chemical Weathering: During the weathering process, rocks may be changed by chemical reactions. In chemical weathering, rock surfaces gradually wear

Mammoth Cave in Kentucky is part of the world's largest cave system. It was formed as acidic water trickled through cracks in limestone, eventually wearing it away.

away in a process called erosion. When raindrops form in clouds, they are made of pure water. But as they fall, they pick up gas particles from the air. When the air is polluted by acidic gases, raindrops become slightly acidic. When this "acid rain"

Did You Know?
Every one thousand years, a mountain loses an average of about 3.5 inches (9 cm) of its height, due to weathering.

falls on a rock, the acidity reacts with minerals in the rock surface, causing it to erode. Normally, weathering only wears down rocks near Earth's surface, but sometimes water soaks down into the ground, causing rocks to erode as far down as 600 feet (185 m). This is how caves are formed.

Physical Weathering: Rocks may also be broken down by physical forces, such as the effects of temperature changes. In the hot deserts, for instance, the sun heats up the rocks during the day. At night, when the air is cold, the rocks freeze. The changing from hot to cold temperatures makes the rocks expand during the day and then shrink at night. As a result, the outer layers of the rocks split and flake off like an onion peel. When it rains, water seeps into the cracks in rocks. If the temperature

The alternate freezing (expansion) and thawing (contraction) of water in cracks can eventually break a large boulder into pieces.

Arches National Park in Utah has more than fifteen hundred rock arches. They have been formed by the faster erosion of soft rock than of surrounding harder rock. The erosion is mainly due to the abrasive effects of windblown sand.

is freezing at night, the frozen water expands and can break apart even the hardest rocks.

Wind Erosion: In desert climates, wind erosion changes the appearance of rocks. The wind blows the loose sand against the rocks. It acts like sandpaper, gradually wearing away the rock surfaces.

Wave Erosion: As ocean waves wash up onshore, sand is constantly being moved to different areas.

Over the centuries, waves crashing against the shore pound away at the rock. The pounding often forms odd and beautiful shapes such as these along the Pacific Coast at Cape Kiwanda State Natural Area in Oregon.

Waves that crash up over the rocks or cliffs break off pieces of rocks. They may carve strange shapes in the rock surfaces. Salt water in the oceans also eats away at the rocks, reshaping them.

Floods: Floods can make serious changes in Earth's landscapes. Rain can exert a lot of force when it hits the ground—a single raindrop can reach speeds of 25 miles (40 km) per hour. Heavy rains, therefore, can wash away anything in their path. Floods can be so strong that they can even loosen up rocks that are firmly

In 2005 mud raced down the hillside in La Conchita, giving residents of this California town little time to escape.

set into the ground. In California, houses that sit on top of hills or cliffs may be destroyed during heavy rainstorms because of mud slides. These occur when the ground becomes so wet that everything near the edge of the hill starts to move quickly downward.

chapter eight

Weather and the Future

Centuries ago, people believed that weather was an unpredictable act of God. It seemed strange and mysterious. Early weather predictions were based on observations of nature—the types and movement of clouds, the direction of the wind, the position of the stars, and even the behavior of animals. These observations were then linked to certain types of weather.

But weather forecasting has become a lot more complicated. Weather experts continue to develop new instruments to study and measure weather conditions. These devices allow forecasters to predict the weather for a short period of time, usually up to a week. Unfortunately, weather is too unpredictable for forecasts to be 100 percent accurate, especially for far in the future.

Tracking the Weather

We have come a long way from ancient weather predictions. Weather forecasting was made easier in

1844, when Samuel Morse invented the electric telegraph so that weather observations could be collected and sent quickly to places far away. Weather information can be gathered more reliably and more quickly through modern technology. Most of this information is gathered by weather observation stations, weather balloons, weather radar, and satellites.

About ten thousand weather reporting stations have been established around the world. Every few hours, these stations collect information on temperature, air pressure, wind direction and speed, humidity, precipitation, and other conditions. The stations then send the information to centers where powerful computers are used to compile the information onto maps. Weather maps help experts to provide forecasts for the day, a

This weather reporting station is on the summit of Mount Washington in New Hampshire. Weather observers have been tracking the weather from this station for more than seventy years.

few days, weeks, and even months in the future. However, many different things can affect the weather, so short-range forecasts are much more reliable than long-range forecasts. Sometimes the constantly changing weather makes it difficult to accurately predict even short-range forecasts.

Weather radar is often used to collect information about precipitation such as rain and snow. Radar sends out radio waves. These radio waves pass through clouds but bounce off raindrops or ice particles. The shortest radio waves produce a strong echo from clouds but are easily absorbed by precipitation. Longer waves are not absorbed but produce a weaker cloud echo. If the precipitation is moving toward or away from the radar, the wavelength of the returning signal will change slightly. This shift, called the Doppler effect, tells observers where weather systems are moving.

This is a portable Doppler radar that is used to track weather. It can be packed into a group of trailerlike containers and shipped worldwide for use in remote sites.

Weather balloons are also used in forecasting the weather. These balloons, carrying measuring and transmitting instruments, are sent up into the

"Under the Weather"

Have you ever heard people say, "I'm a little under the weather today," when they are not feeling very well? Weather conditions actually can influence people's moods and even their physical health. A bright sunny day can make us feel happy and optimistic, while low pressure and high humidity can make people irritable. In various parts of the world, people feel irritable and ill when certain winds blow. These "ill winds" include siroccos—hot, dry, dusty winds that blow from North Africa into southern Europe; the hot, dry winds called foehns in the Alps; and the chinooks that blow in the eastern Rockies in North America. In Israel 25 percent of the population suffers from headaches, upset stomachs, and breathing problems when a hot wind called the *sharav* blows. Doctors believe that the illness associated with certain weather conditions may be caused by changes in the electrical characteristics of the air that occur when these winds are blowing.

upper atmosphere. We know that most of our weather occurs in the lowest level of the atmosphere, the troposphere. So why study the upper atmosphere? Because the weather that takes place in the troposphere is influenced by the layers above it. We need to study the upper layers to understand what is going on in the lowest layer.

Weather balloons carrying meteorlogical instruments are used to measure temperature, pressure, humidity, and winds.

Weather balloons filled with helium or hydrogen carry an instrument called a radiosonde. The radiosonde takes various measurements of the atmosphere: the temperature, air pressure, and humidity of air at different levels. The information is then sent back to weather stations through a radio transmitter. When weather balloons float up to about 90,000 feet (17 miles, or 27 km), they burst. Then a parachute attached to the radiosonde opens and brings the device safely to the ground.

Weather satellites orbit Earth to collect weather information. Satellites carry television cameras that take pictures of Earth. These send signals to weather stations on the ground so they can produce these photographs. By studying them, meteorologists can spot hurricanes and other dangerous storms. This allows the weather service to issue warnings to people threatened by these storms. Satellites can also take measurements of temperatures on the ground,

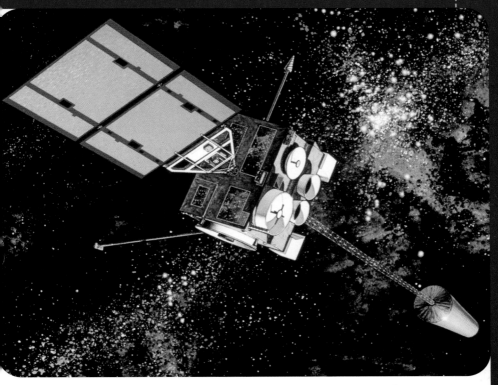

The United States has two orbiting weather satellites that collect weather data and send it back to Earth for meteorologists to use.

on the sea surface, and at different levels of the atmosphere. They can also determine the direction and speed of the wind and the humidity in the air.

Airplanes and ships also provide weather information. Some airplanes have instruments that record the wind direction and speed and the air temperature, then transmit the information through satellites. Special weather ships and weather buoys, as well as merchant ships, can provide weather information at sea level. Weather rockets are also sent out into the atmosphere and then radio back information to weather centers.

Can We Control the Weather?

We are constantly trying to predict the weather, but how about controlling it? In 1946 scientists discovered how to alter such weather conditions as rain, fog, hail, hurricanes, and lightning. In a process called cloud seeding, airplanes drop particles such as silver iodide or dry ice (frozen carbon dioxide) into

Weather Lore

Ancient people made some important connections between their observations of nature and weather. We often use some of this old weather lore to help forecast the weather. While most weather lore is helpful and reliable, some is not.

"Red sky at night, sailors' delight; Red sky in morning, sailors take warning." This old saying is true. The red color comes from sunlight reflected off clouds. A red sunset in the evening is usually a sign of good weather because weather usually moves from west to east, and the west horizon must be clear for reflection to occur. A red sunrise means that bad weather is on the way because the sunlight is reflected off rain clouds moving in from the west.

cumulonimbus clouds that cause the tiny water droplets to condense into raindrops.

Cloud seeding has been used in the United States, France, Russia, and Australia. It can be used to increase rainfall in dry regions. However, moisture-soaked clouds must be in the area to produce rain. Cloud seeding can also break up fog at airports. It reduces the energy that builds up in clouds and, therefore, has

Frogs can predict rainy weather. They love dampness. Before it rains, the air is humid, so the frogs will be out.

A pinecone's scales open up in very dry weather and close shut when it is damp outside before a rain.

You can tell a storm is coming by watching animals: Birds fly low in the sky. Horses, cows, and sheep become restless and move in close together. Frogs croak loudly and stay in the water. Cats and dogs get restless. The hair on your pets may stand up because of the electrical charge in the air.

Groundhog Day is an old tradition in the United States. It is said that if a groundhog sees its shadow on February 2, there will be six more weeks of winter. The groundhog's weather forecast, however, is not very reliable.

This plane is equipped with cloud seeding equipment.

been able to weaken storm clouds, including hurricanes. In Russia the size of damaging hailstones has been greatly reduced.

Scientists hope someday to control the weather to prevent disastrous floods and dangerous droughts. Science-fiction writers have pictured future worlds where it rains precisely on schedule, in just the right places to water crops, fill reservoirs, and keep life from getting too boring. But weather is so changeable that even with the latest technology, we may never achieve that kind of power over the tremendous forces that drive Earth's weather machine.

Rainy Weekends

Does it seem like it is more likely to rain on a weekend, when you are planning a picnic or some other outdoor fun, than it does during the week? Meteorologists have discovered that this weather pattern really exists on the East Coast of the United States. Analyzing weather data back to 1946, they found that the most precipitation occurs on Saturdays and the least on Mondays. There is a logical reason for this. During the week, people riding in cars and buses to work and school produce pollution. The air pollution levels hit a peak on Saturdays and reach a weekly low by Monday. The pollution absorbs heat, and the hot air rises, forming clouds. Tiny particles in the pollution serve as seeds around which moisture condenses, producing rain.

Glossary

air masses: portions of the atmosphere that move around Earth's surface

air pressure: the pushing force exerted by the molecules of the atmosphere; also called atmospheric pressure

altocumulus: medium-level clouds shaped like round heaps, patches, or rows

altostratus: medium-level clouds in thin sheets that cover the sky

aneroid barometer: an instrument that measures air pressure

atmosphere: a mixture of gases, including nitrogen, oxygen, carbon dioxide, and water vapor, that surrounds Earth

axis: an imaginary line extending through Earth, from one pole to the other, around which the planet rotates

blizzard: a severe snowstorm with strong, cold winds

cirrocumulus: cirrus clouds that form patchy clumps

cirrostratus: cirrus clouds that form thin, white sheets

cirrus: thin, white, feathery clouds; also called mare's tails

climate: the pattern of weather conditions typical of a particular area over time

clouds: masses of tiny water droplets or ice crystals suspended in the atmosphere

cold front: cold air that is moving into an area of warm air

condensation: the passage of a gas, such as water vapor, into a liquid or solid state as the temperature is lowered

convection currents: circular movements of air (or fluid) caused by the rising of warm air and the falling of cool air

Coriolis effect: a westward shift of the winds blowing from the poles toward the equator, due to Earth's rotation

cumulonimbus: low, dark cumulus storm clouds; also called thunderheads

cumulus: clouds that appear piled up into heaps

cyclone: a popular synonym for tornado. In meteorology it refers to a large weather system with a circular wind movement and low pressure at the center.

desert: a dry region that gets very little rain

dew point: the temperature at which water vapor in the air condenses onto dust particles, forming visible droplets of water

doldrums: a usually mild, calm belt of rising air at the equator, between the trade winds

Doppler effect: the shift in frequency (and wavelength) of light, sound, or radio waves bounced back from a moving object

El Niño: a cyclic change in the world's weather patterns due to a change in the direction of the winds and ocean currents in the Pacific Ocean

equinox: the day when the lengths of daylight and darkness are equal. It occurs twice each year, in the spring (vernal equinox) and fall (autumnal equinox).

erosion: wearing away of Earth's surface by the action of water or wind

evaporation: a change of state from a liquid to a gas

fog: a cloud that touches the ground

fossil fuel: a material used as energy sources, such as coal, oil, and gas, formed from the remains of ancient organisms buried under rock

front: the area where two moving air masses meet

frost: water vapor frozen solid into tiny ice crystals

garúa: a special kind of clear, very wet fog found along the coast of Peru and Chile

general circulation: air that circulates over the entire Earth

glacier: a large mass of ice covering an extensive area of land or water and formed from the accumulation of snow over many years

global warming: a worldwide increase in Earth's average temperature

gravity: a force of attraction between objects; in particular, the force that keeps the atmosphere and objects from drifting away from Earth

greenhouse effect: a warming of Earth due to atmospheric gases such as carbon dioxide, which trap heat like the glass in a greenouse

Gulf Stream: a warm ocean current that flows from the Gulf of Mexico to the North Atlantic

hail: precipitation of tiny balls of ice condensed from water droplets in clouds. Pellets of hail are called hailstones.

hibernation: a sleeplike state of inactivity in which some animals, such as bears, pass the winter

highs: high-pressure systems, in which winds from high altitudes blow down toward Earth's surface and bring calm, clear weather

horse latitudes: belts of very still air at the boundaries between the trade winds and the prevailing westerlies

Humboldt Current: a cold ocean current that flows up the western coast of South America

hurricane: a violent tropical storm with circular winds surrounding a low-pressure zone of calm air, called the eye

ice ages: periods when Earth experiences extremely cold weather and much of its surface is covered by snow and ice

interglacial period: a time of warmer temperatures between ice ages

jet streams: winds in the tropopause that follow regular paths

kinetic energy: energy of motion; the hotter a molecule, the greater its kinetic energy and the faster it moves

latitude: a measure of the distance from the equator toward the poles along the curved surface of Earth, expressed in degrees of a circle

lightning: a sudden discharge of electricity within or from a cloud, producing a brilliant flash of light

lows: low-pressure systems, in which rising, swirling warm air currents form clouds and bring unstable, stormy weather

meteorologist: a scientist who studies weather

migration: seasonal travels of certain birds and mammals between two regions

migratory high-pressure systems: highs that move from west to east

millibars (mb): units of air pressure

monsoon: seasonal heavy rain that occurs in India and other parts of Asia

nimbostratus: thick, dark clouds that usually bring rain or snow

orbit: the oval path traveled by Earth as it revolves around the sun

ozone: a highly reactive form of oxygen containing three oxygen molecules. In the atmosphere, it traps part of the energy from sunlight.

particulates: soot, ash, and other solid particles that are a component of air pollution

photosynthesis: a process in which plants and certain bacteria use sunlight energy to convert carbon dioxide and water to complex carbon compounds used as food and building materials. Oxygen is produced as a by-product.

polar easterlies: the belts of prevailing winds closest to the poles

polar zones: the areas around the North and South Poles, the coldest regions on Earth

precipitation: condensation of water vapor in the atmosphere to a liquid or solid state so that it falls to Earth's surface in the form of rain, snow, or hail

prevailing westerlies: the belts of prevailing winds north and south of the trade winds

prevailing winds: winds that blow in the same direction all year round

radiosonde: an instrument carried up into the upper atmosphere by a weather balloon to transmit weather measurements back to the ground by radio

rain: water vapor condensed into drops of liquid water that fall from clouds

sleet: precipitation in the form of tiny balls of ice or a mixture of rain and ice

smog: a mixture of fog and pollutants that can be irritating or even deadly

snow: an accumulation of snowflakes falling to or lying on Earth's surface

snowflakes: complex structures formed from ice crystals into which water vapor condenses when a cloud reaches freezing temperatures

solstice: the time of year when the daylight period is the shortest and the darkness is the longest (the winter solstice) or the daylight period is the longest and the darkness is the shortest (the summer solstice)

storm: a weather disturbance that may include strong winds, precipitation (rain, hail, sleet, or snow), and thunder and lightning

stratocumulus: rounded clouds that look joined together into a low sheet

stratosphere: the layer of atmosphere just beyond the troposphere

stratus: clouds that look like thin sheets

subtropical zones: regions between the temperate and tropical zones, which have warm temperatures for most of the year

temperate zones: regions that typically have warm summers, cold winters, and rain and snow

thunder: the sound wave produced by the explosion of air molecules heated by a bolt of lightning

tornado: an extremely violent storm in the form of a funnel of spinning air

trade winds: belts of prevailing winds just north and south of the equator

tropical zones: regions near the equator, which are hot all year round

tropics: hot regions at and near the equator

tropopause: the boundary between the troposphere and stratosphere, the two innermost layers of the atmosphere

troposphere: the innermost and densest layer of the atmosphere, containing the air we breathe

typhoon: a hurricane in the western Pacific Ocean or the China Sea; also refers to a violent storm in India

warm front: warm air that is moving into an area of cold air

water cycle: the successive processes of evaporation, condensation, and precipitation that keep water circulating between Earth's surface and the atmosphere

water vapor: water in the gas state, formed by the evaporation of liquid water

weather: the condition of the atmosphere at a particular time

weathering: changes in the landscape produced by the action of wind and water

winds: moving air masses

Bibliography

Bramwell, Martyn. *Earth Science Library: Weather.* New York: Franklin Watts, 1997.

Burnie, David. *How Nature Works.* Pleasantville, NY: The Reader's Digest Association, Inc., 1991.

Christian, Spencer, and Antonia Felix. *Can It Really Rain Frogs?* New York: John Wiley & Sons, Inc., 1997.

Cosgrove, Brian. *Eyewitness Books: Weather.* New York: Alfred A. Knopf, 1991.

Davies, Kay, and Wendy Oldfield. *The Super Science Book of Weather.* New York: Thomson Learning, 1993.

Farndon, John. *Eyewitness Explorers: Weather.* New York: Dorling Kindersley, Inc., 1992.

Ford, Adam. *Weather Watch.* New York: Lothrop, Lee, & Shepard Books, 1981.

Galan, Mark. *Understanding Science & Nature: Weather & Climate.* Alexandria, VA: Time-Life Books, 1993.

Hardy, Ralph. *Teach Yourself: Weather.* Chicago, IL: NTC Publishing Group, 1996.

Kandel, Robert. *Our Changing Climate.* New York: McGraw-Hill, Inc., 1990.

Nash, J. Madeleine. "The Fury of El Nino." *Time Magazine,* February 16, 1998, 67-73.

Time Life Student Library: Planet Earth. Alexandria, VA: Time-Life Books, 1997.

Wilson, Francis, and Felicity Mansfield. *Spotter's Guide to the Weather.* New York: Mayflower Books, 1979.

For Further Information

Books

Aguado, Edward, and James E. Burt. *Understanding Weather and Climate.* Upper Saddle River, NJ: Pearson Prentice Hall, 2003.

Chart Studio. *Weather and Climate Workbook: Real Science Made Easy.* Berkeley, CA: Silver Dolphin Books, 2005.

Cox, John D. *Weather for Dummies.* New York: Hungry Minds, Inc., 2000.

Goldstein, Mel. *The Complete Idiot's Guide to Weather.* Indianapolis, IN: Alpha Books, 2002.

Padilla, Michael J., Ioannis Miaoulis, and Martha Cyr. *Prentice Hall Science Explorer: Weather and Climate.* Upper Saddle River, NJ: Pearson Prentice Hall, 2006.

Rupp, Rebecca. *Weather!* North Adams, MA: Storey Publishing, 2003.

Taylor, Barbara. *Weather and Climate: Geography Facts and Experiments.* New York: Kingfisher, 2002.

Vogt, Gregory L. *The Atmosphere.* Minneapolis, MN: Twenty-First Century Books, 2007.

Vogt, Gregory L. *The Lithosphere.* Minneapolis, MN: Twenty-First Century Books, 2007.

Winner, Cherie. *Life in the Tundra: Alaska's Coastal Plain.* Minneapolis, MN: Twenty-First Century Books, 2003.

Web Sites

The EPA Global Warming Site
http://www.epa.gov/globalwarming/
This site features information about climate change and the greenhouse effect.

Franklin's Forecast
http://www.fi.edu/weather/
Simple explanations and movie clips of weather events, radar, and weather satellites are featured on this site, as well as how to make your own weather station, in-depth features on topics of special interest such as El Niño. It also offers huge numbers of links to other weather sites and web pages with information on tornadoes, hurricanes, lightning, weather careers, and other weather topics.

Hurricane and Natural Disaster Brochures
http://www.aoml.noaa.gov/general/lib/hurricbro.html
Information from the National Oceanic and Atmospheric Administration and the National Weather Service on hurricanes, tornadoes, heat waves, floods, and weather reconnaissance can be found on this web site.

PSC Meteorology Program Cloud Boutique
http://vortex.plymouth.edu/clouds.html
This site has cloud descriptions and pictures.

Theater of Electricity
http://www.mos.org/sln/toe/toe.html
This site has illustrated highlights of Museum of Science exhibits, such as "Touching Lightning" and "Franklin's Kite," plus a safety quiz, resources, and video and picture galleries.

United States Interactive Climate Pages
http://www.cdc.noaa.gov/USclimate/
On this site, you can find climate maps for the entire United States, going back to 1895, and climate maps for individual cities. It also has a glossary of terms and links to climate sites.

Weather and Climate Science
http://www.usatoday.com/weather/climate/
USA Today text and graphics on various weather phenomena, including winds, storms, and El Niño, can be found on this web site..

Index

Photo Acknowledgments

About the Authors

Dr. Alvin Silverstein is a former professor of biology and director of the Physician Assistant Program at the College of Staten Island of the City University of New York. Virginia B. Silverstein is a translator of Russian scientific literature.

The Silversteins' collaboration began with a biochemical research project at the University of Pennsylvania. Since then they have produced six children and published more than two hundred books that have received high acclaim for their clear, timely, and authoritative coverage of science and health topics.

Laura Silverstein Nunn, a graduate of Kean College, began helping with the research for her parents' books while she was in high school. Since joining the writing team, she has coauthored more than eighty books.